NEW SKIN: *Poetry and Prayers*

TINA KARAGULIAN

Black Rose Press
San Antonio

Black Rose Press
P.O. Box 6707
San Antonio, TX 78209
www.tinakaragulian.com

Cover, layout, logo, and book design by Tina Karagulian
Photograph on back cover by Marcy Maloy.
Reprinted with permission. www.marcymaloy.com

Karagulian, Tina, 1965–

New Skin : Poetry and Prayers from *It Is Time*, a memoir of
reconciliation embracing various spiritual traditions, healing the
Armenian Genocide and the Feminine Wound, and claiming the call
of a Divine Mother / Tina Karagulian

ISBN: 978-0-983804222

1. Poetry 2. Spirituality

Printed in the United States of America on recycled paper.

This book is dedicated to Paschal Booker and Diana Der-Hovanessian, two of my favorite poets.

Table of Contents

She

A drop of light,
the touch of sun,
is but a taste
of the fullness
of Her,
a river of longing
finally quenched.
When I but turn
my head,
like a sunflower
toward Her warmth,
my heart is filled
by Her plenty.
I need not whisper
nor speak—
the smallest desires
of my soul are heard,
and I realize
that they always were.
Such love
cannot be contained
in form
yet explodes from it—
human language,
gesture, silent nudge
all bow and yield
to pure intention,
yet also rest within
every weakness.
She guides my step,
ignites my spark,
and we claim
each other
as One.

Divine Mother

Exalted Mother in All Forms,
Enter and explode my heart,
Guide me in right action,
That I may be your eyes,
That I may hear with your ears,
That my soul may rest upon you
and love with commanding presence,
Within every thought,
Within every action,
Knowing, without doubt,
That you are my Divine Mother,
You protect me as a Warrior
Walks without fear into darkness,
You nurture my soul's stirrings, and
You adore me with a love that
Surpasses human understanding.
I fully claim you,
and I am forever yours. [1]

Longing

Tenderly, my six-year-old hands
pushed the chair
to the kitchen cabinet.
I climbed up and reached for a glass,
a container to hold not only
the juice I poured,
but a vessel that would
hold your grief,
your wistfulness.

Too many goodbyes
had been shared
by family members,
often not by choice.
I knew that every goodbye
would hearken back to 1915.

I yearned to ease your sadness,
your longing.
I offered you communion,
with the juice of oranges.

You smiled amidst your tears,
and for one moment,
I believed my love
could wipe away your pain,
could erase the mark of genocide,
could turn your face toward the sun.
But your sorrow was always too great.

You could not see me
past the burden you carried.

I believed my prayers
would pay off some day,
that the ley lines of loss
firmly etched into your bosom
would erode by pure love—
but it never seemed enough.
You could not see
how much I ached for you.

I became witness,
as therapist and spiritual seeker,
put words to wordless moments,
offered a sacred space
for others to discover,
to piece together,
to find voice.

Yet I left a piece
of my soul behind,
waiting,
praying,
for my mother,
my family,
my culture,
to find peace.

I continue to pray,
envisioning that moment
of completeness,
when we can join
one another
inside the fullness.

The Right of Your Passage

Taste the next step,
into the wonder of soul-knowing,
the peaceful strength,
the confidence of self,
the excitement of adventures yet in store;
This is what awaits you,
you are shorn of all that did not fulfill you,
and your presence in our lives
is a pure and sweet blessing.
Continue to share your journey with us,
for we are ever grateful for the beauty that is you.

Jagadakeer*

Was it fate that led us through desert sand,
 in broken moonlight,
  where whispered dreams floated toward distant stars?

Was it fate that chiseled families into puzzle pieces,
 led away "by choice", in a "relocation package"
  complete with all the amenities any genocide can offer?

Was it fate that unanswered prayers remained poised
 in cellular memory, awaiting release only in the
  presence of true witness?

The poetry of my fate pierces through prisms of soul,
 Triumphant in the language of true ancestry.[2]

Jagadakeer is the Armenian word for *writing on the
 forehead* or fate.

Still-born

I had a stillborn—the priesthood.
A calling that lived and died in my womb,
in the darkness of my heart.
It never had a chance
to see the light of day.
It never had a chance to take
its first breath.
I know many women
have had the same loss,
had to hide the death
of their hearts
so that others could live,
so that the world could
go on and continue
with their plans,
with their visions.
I feel I was born
to be,
to express,
to give,
to lead,
with parts of my soul
that never had a chance to shine.
Maybe the new that is to come,
will use all the gifts I have held back.
Maybe it means
that I am being led
to an inclusive priesthood.
That is the hope:
Born—
in the Stillness.

See-faring

I came from the sea,
much like Aphrodite
in a tumble of wave,
unseen amid the foam;
it rose up,
and I could feel no ground.
Carried into
the brine
of a bigger Mother,
who claimed me
as Her own,
once more I tumbled,
mingling breath
with salt,
until I was spit up,
baptized through and through,
by the waters
of my Living God.
My heart remembers
my emergence:
my skin became supple,
my eyes revealed new sight.
I was remade,
whole.
I tasted a promise
of sustenance
until I am,
once again,
submerged,
reunited,
into the salted wine
of My Beloved.

Community

I imagine
that during the genocide,
my grandmother
walked on hot sand,
lost and betrayed
by her neighborhood community,
wondering how
this came to pass.

I imagine
that in her daze,
she could not see,
a community
of animals in the desert,
walking beside her,
peering up at her,
sending her encouragement
and strength.

I imagine
a band of angels,
encircling her,
ministering
to her broken heart.

I imagine
God's tenderness
shining
amid brutal acts,
opening hearts
of unlikely heroes.

I imagine
that for every community
that denies a soul,
many more communities
scramble to retrieve,
to nurture,
and to mend
its severed remnants.

And as it comes together,
piece by piece,
we begin to see
the woven threads
of so many loved ones
smiling upon us.

When we see them,
we realize
that they have *always*
been with us,
that they have *always*
sustained us.

We come *full circle*—
yet it never ends,
rippling out,
melting
into the vastness

we
imagine.

Crossroads

I see this moment
of my life
unfolding,
showing me
the mountains and valleys
that I have traveled,
stories that I have carried—
both yours and mine—
on my back,
in my belly,
and in my womb.
I needed rest,
a place
to assemble the words and images,
all shapes and sizes of them,
like multi-colored glass marbles
shining in the sunlight,
reflecting my inner and outer world
back to me.
I needed time
to collect them,
unite them,
and rinse them in cool water,
then watch them
dry out on the shore.
I needed to know they
belonged somewhere,
that their journey
was not wasted,
that they have
a lightness of purpose,
a spark of love,

and a belly of humor,
wrapped up in wisdom
for a hopeful future.
I offer
these blessed gems,
for the roads
they have traversed,
and for the rest
they have found;
they have become
the river bed,
the ocean floor,
the foundation
for the One Voice
I now claim.

A Touch

I wipe your face,
and in your sweat and pain,
I am tempted to stay in suffering—
yours and my own.

Yet I hear you call me,
beyond myself.
The moment I touch you,
you take me beyond this moment,
teaching me
that *all* fearful thoughts
tempt us,
attack our minds,
steal our spirit.

But you show me the way,
in the moment of that touch—
and all the earth stood still.

You walk beside me,
guiding me
through the dark waters
of my mind,
in the broken bones
of my body.

You promise *never* to leave me,
whenever I walk this walk,
for suffering is never
the end,
never the destination.

You offer me peace—
my birthright—
if I but touch your face,
and face each fear
with quiet calm.

Death, suffering,
can never stop
heaven on earth—
we must resurrect ourselves
to our true destiny,
beyond moments—
beyond roles we play—
beyond pain of illusion—
and beyond the tenderness
of my touch.

I know now
that I *can*
step into my resurrection.

Whenever I yearn to touch you,
I allow you to touch my soul—
and then I can claim
my true lineage:

For
I Am
Living Daughter
of my Living God.

The Annunciation of My Soul

Meeting of two wondrous beings!
You, oh messenger of light,
swift on wing,
you sought out
the physical incarnation of the
Divine Feminine Mother God,
who long ago
chose Mary as her vessel,
to birth Unconditional Love
in a new way—
for Divine Mother
is the Ultimate Creator,
the Holy Spirit that whispered
through your words, Gabriel,
planted a seed in you, Mary,
and was birthed in you, Christ.
May she speak, plant, and birth
Her unending love
within the depths of my soul.[3]

My Heart is Full

And you, daughters of my soul,
have no fear[*]—
authentic self,
babe in new skin,
transparent heart,
wrapped in curvatures of hills,
held in the crooks of your valleys,
from Zeitun to where my heart lives,
there is no distance: **seerdus letzoon eh.** [**]
I walk with women who know this terrain,
who turn back and beckon me
across the threshold.
Mother of My Soil,
you call me inside the beat of drums
to bridge my inner worlds.
Now no one place is more real.
I plant my roots inside your bosom,
ever complete.[4]

[*]Reference to the Bible passage from Ruth 3:11
[**]Armenian translation of *my heart is full.*

All Matter of Communion

I see altars and communion everywhere now—
the amniotic sac
a suspended place
where communion travels
through nourishing liquids
of an umbilical cord.

I watch the moment when
a woman bends her nipple,
ever so gently,
into the mouth of her babe,
much like the goblet of wine
is tipped so that we can drink.

I see our crossing guard
wave and smile to passing motorists,
offering a good morning greeting
to each child she guides,
and as they cross the street,
with her protective hand held high—
they have been blessed
by the richness of her communion.

I watch a female cardinal
bend her orange beak
to her fiery red partner,
giving him not only seed
but a lot of love thrown in.

I notice when one offers a flower,
a piece of fruit,
or a smile to another—

I see the offering transform
the face of the other,
in quiet wonder.

I marvel at all the altars
and passing of communion
that take place
within each moment,
within each day.

And in case we forget
that God is infinite in Her giving,
She enjoys dropping another surprise our way,
like a love note you put in someone's lunch,
and all we need do,
is notice.

It Is Time

You are the fruit of all my loss—
You take my heart to the valley in Zeitun,
where ripe olives burst in your mouth.
You are my life,
which continues to live through you.
No desert can take away my longing
to find you,
to love you.
I *could not* rest until all was put right,
through you,
through my children's children.
Such is a mother's love—
Anger and hate cannot consume it.
Our souls are bolder,
brighter,
and more resilient than hate.
I—am—your—grandmother!
You are my blood,
my heart,
My Zeitun Warrior.
Pure strength and love—
this is our legacy.
My insistent voice is the voice of all mothers
who fight to hear and to be heard.
Your mother yearned for me through you.
I could not fully see or hear your mother.
I feared losing her, too.
Many of us did that.
That was not living.
It is time to unleash that fear.
You are so *very* loved.
No one is left out,

not you,
not your mother,
and not any Turkish woman or man.
God's love is big enough for everyone.
Guh hasgunas?
Do you understand?
Ayoh, guh hasgunam.
Yes, I understand.
I am the proudest woman,
watching my own flesh and blood
heal what I could not.

It Is Time.[5]

Bending Into

Do I dare say yes
to the One who waits upon
my every whisper?

Do I dare say yes
to the Holy Kiss
and breath
that scatter all doubt?

Do I dare say yes
as I stand upon
my inner cliffs of longing?

Do I dare walk into
unknown waters
with my Living God?

Do I dare rest
into the yes
of my own resurrection?

Dwelling

Loving Mother, Christ—
Make a space within my heart
to feel your touch upon me,
your hand upon my forehead,
your signature upon my thoughts,
your words upon my lips.
Help me to sit still and wait upon you,
to earnestly move toward you,
to be filled by all that you give.
Help me to remain—
not to rush off
to take care of other things
before fully receiving you.
Steady me,
Hold me,
Fill me
with your infinite peace.
Show me how to bless
and to love myself,
so that I can share that
blessing with others.

Come—stay at my home.

Amen.[6]

New Skin

At times we wear the skins of
caretaker, tender listener, and
supporter of others' dreams and visions—
so that they may thrive on their intended roads.

At times we walk alongside
the death and suffering of others,
so that they may not feel alone,
so that love's true essence may revive and resurrect.

Yet when we courageously enter the darkness
of our deepest fears and unanswered dreams—
then the true alchemy begins:

With new eyes we see the needs and wants
that clamor for our attention,
and begin to let go
of unnecessary obligations.

We learn to quiet all the voices that tempt
and taunt us from inner peace,
releasing the hold they have
within our bodies and minds.

We walk steadfastly into our center,
allowing for the One True Voice
to emerge and guide,
daily surrendering to Her wisdom.

We listen inside voiceless places of our heart,
until the silence spurs us into action
that feeds our deepest reserves.

We feel the vulnerability of new skin,
yet allow its sleekness to breathe us.

For our every weakness
we receive increasing compassion
that naturally ripples out
and envelopes others.

Each time we focus our attention
on *our* soul's vision,
the warrior within stands tall,
protecting a newly emerging creativity
that is initially unrecognizable,
peacefully familiar,
yet strongly resolute.

Once we claim the wild voice of our soul,
there's no turning back.

Bibliography and Notes

[1]Tina Karagulian, Prayer to *Divine Mother*, (San Antonio: Black Rose Press), 2008.

[2]Tina Karagulian, *Jagadakeer* in *Insights on the Journey: Trauma, Healing, & Wholeness, An Anthology of Women's Writing*, compiled by Maureen Leach, OSF, (San Antonio: peaceCENTER), 2008, 39.

[3]Tina Karagulian, *The Annunciation of My Soul*, originally in *Lifting Women's Voices: Prayers to Change the World*, Margaret Rose, Jenny Te Paa, Jeanne Person, and Abagail Nelson, editors, (New York: Morehouse Publishing), 2009, 171.

[4]Tina Karagulian, *My Heart is Full*, in *Sustaining Abundant Life*, (San Antonio: The Episcopal Diocese of West Texas Education Department), 2009, 21. Ruth 3:11, *The New Oxford Annotated Bible with the Apocrypha*, Edited by Herbert G. May and Bruce M. Metzger, (New York: Oxford University Press), 1977, 328.

[5]Tina Karagulian and her grandmother Zarman Meguerditchian, *It Is Time*, (San Antonio: Black Rose Press), 2011.

[6]Tina Karagulian, Mother's Day sermon, The Episcopal Church of Reconciliation, San Antonio, Texas, May 9, 2010.